DREAM PLAN PURSUE

Australian Aboriginal Dot Art

Create your very own Aboriginal Dot Painting using a cotton swab (Q-tip). Simply dot water colors or washable paint into the shape of your favorite characters until it is all filled.

Materials:

- coloring page
- water colors or washable paint
- cotton swabs

Instructions:

- Select your coloring page
- Dip a cotton swab in the paint and dab it on the coloring page
- Use a new cotton swab for each color

If you do not have paint available, use crayons or markers for a similar effect. Happy coloring!!!

Tommy is learning to change a tire.

Tommy's Dream Car

United States of America Flag

Australian Flag

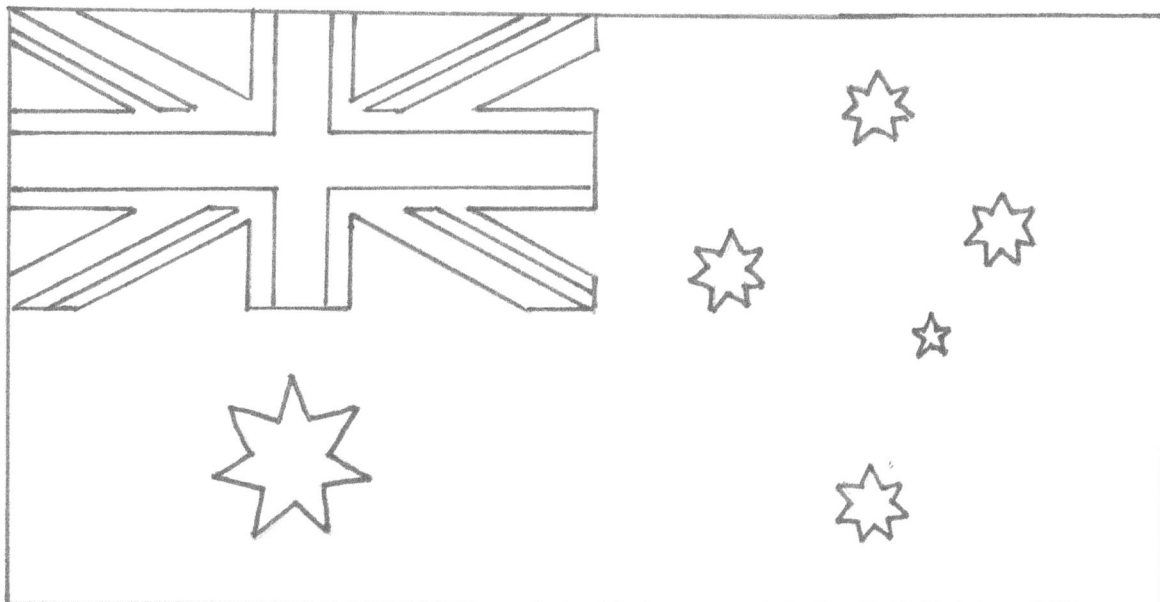

Color and Compare the Flags

Patty Sue's dreams come true!

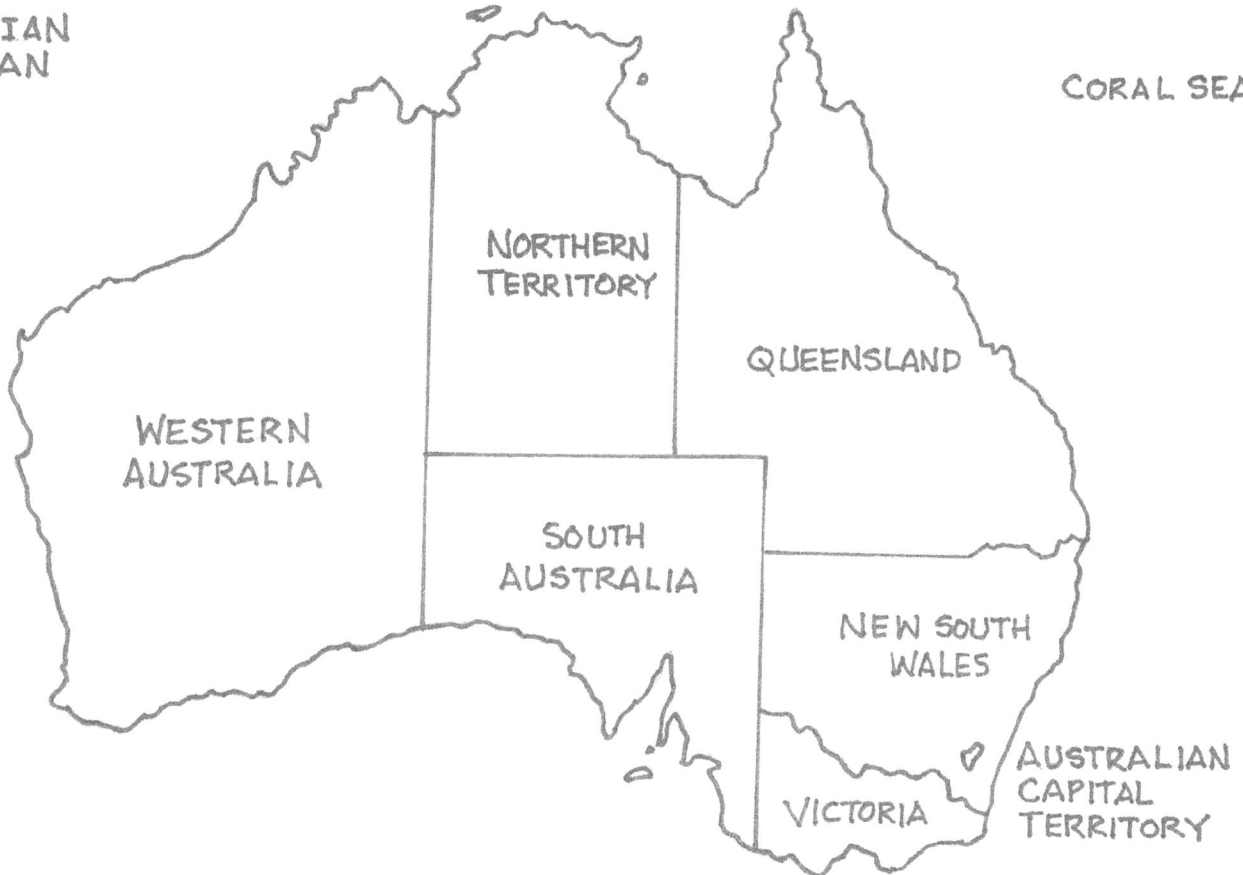

INDIAN
OCEAN

CORAL SEA

NORTHERN
TERRITORY

QUEENSLAND

WESTERN
AUSTRALIA

SOUTH
AUSTRALIA

NEW SOUTH
WALES

AUSTRALIAN
CAPITAL
TERRITORY

INDIAN
OCEAN

VICTORIA

TASMANIA

Australia
Where Patty and her friends live.

Dr. Darnell Dingo pursues his dream.

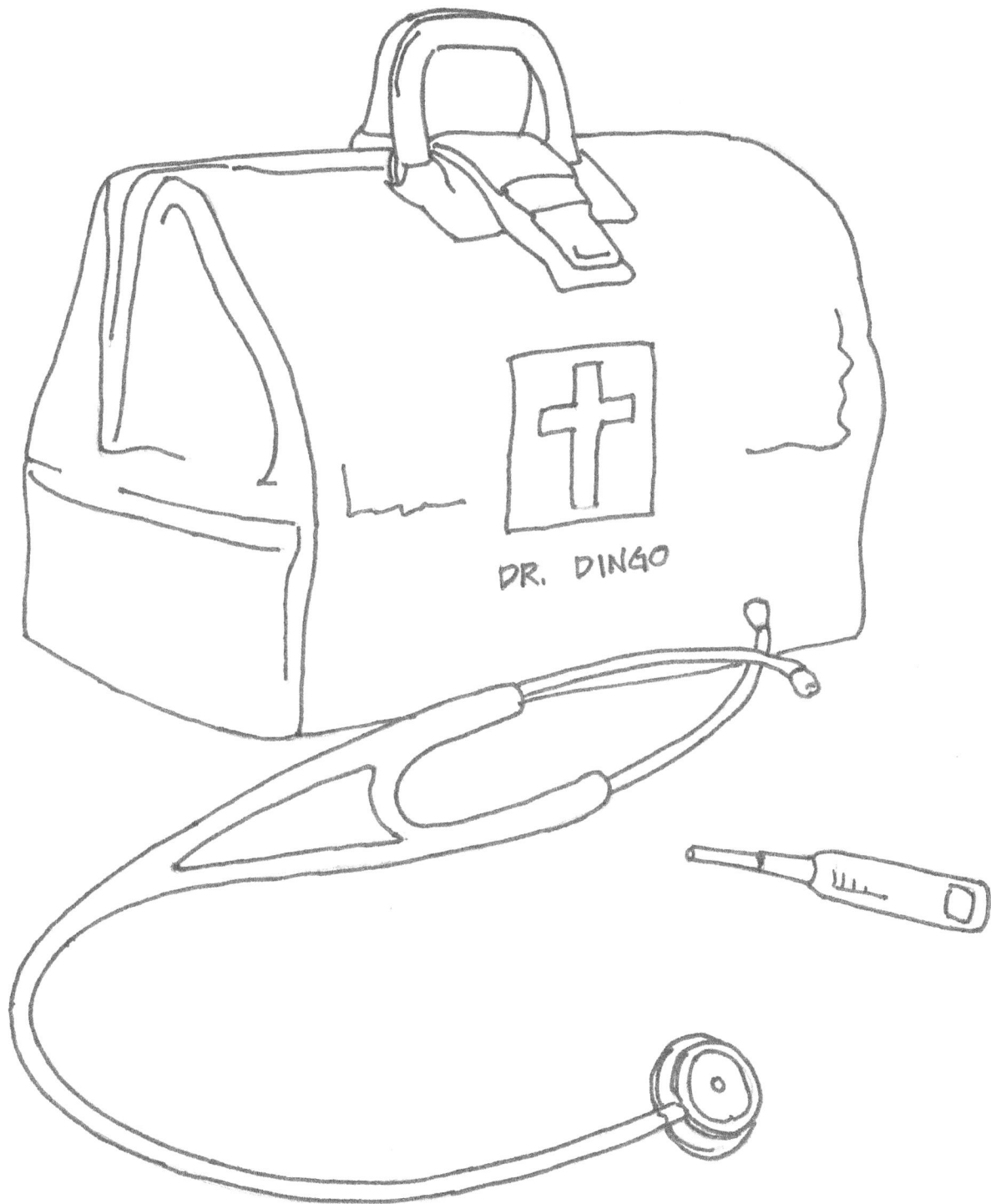

Learn about other
Australian animals.

Karl knows practice is important
to reach his dream.

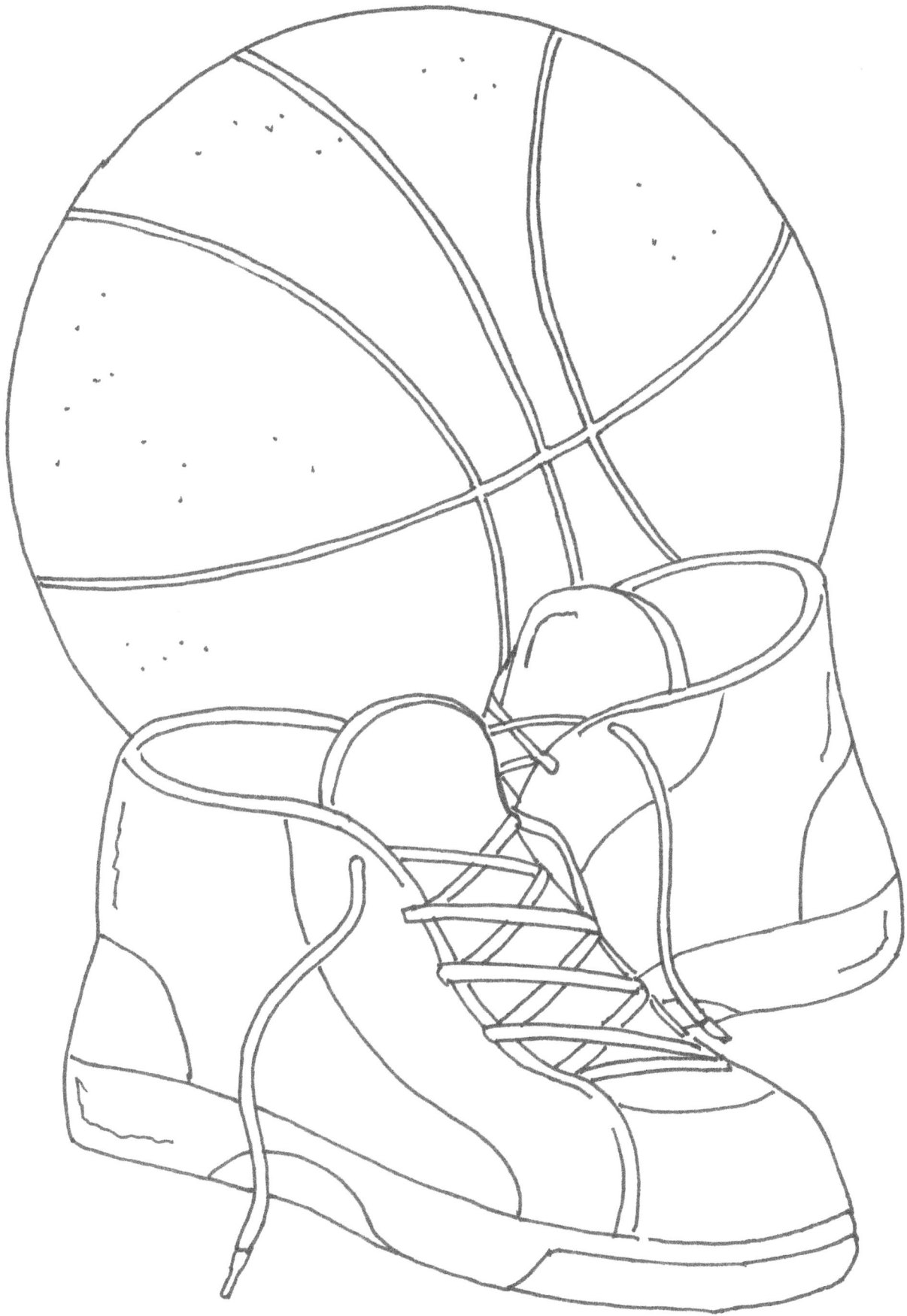

Selena plans her meal.

Selena's Kitchen

Do sharks dream big, too?

Ona practices in pursuit of her dream.

Which instrument was designed by
the aboriginal people of Australia?

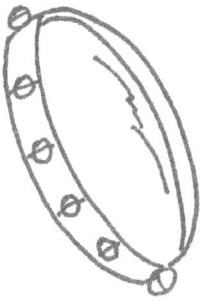

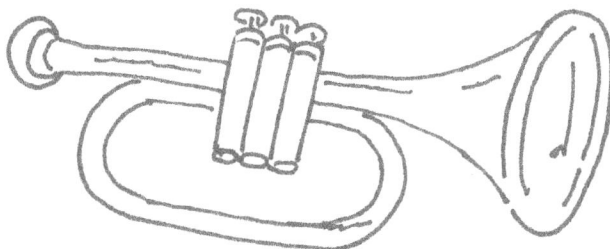

Patty Sue and her pals will meet a new friend in book two.
Who will it be?